W9-CSL-076

Summer Wild
PRODUCTIONS

and

Bob Herger & **Ken Budd**

are thrilled to share their creation,

VANCOUVER
Living the Moment

A Photographic Essay of Metro Vancouver

Metro Vancouver has once again been thrust into the spotlight at the centre of the world's stage. During this unique time in its history as host of the 2010 Olympic and Paralympic Winter Games, it is worthy of praise. We hope our goal to produce the quintessential photographic study of this outstanding region has been achieved.

Our thematic focus for the project, *The People, Their Places and Their Pleasures,* meant that we were destined to meet hundreds of proud residents, all who were incredibly generous in assisting with our quest. Giving seems to be a trait of those who get to call this magnificent area home. This publication could be dedicated to the spirit of that giving.

Enjoy it and cherish living your moments.

Bob Herger

Ken Budd

Smythe Works
ASSOCIATES

and

Bob Herger & Ken Budd

are thrilled to share their creation,

VANCOUVER
Living the Moment

Metro Vancouver has once again been thrust into the spotlight at the centre of the world's stage. During this unique time in its history as host of the 2010 Olympic and Paralympic Winter Games, it is worthy of praise. We hope our goal to produce the quintessential photographic study of this outstanding region has been achieved.

Our thematic focus for the project, The People, Their Places and Their Pleasures, meant that we were destined to meet hundreds of proud residents, all who were incredibly generous in assisting with our quest. Giving seems to be a trait of those who get to call this magnificent area home. This publication could be dedicated to the spirit of that giving.

Enjoy it and cherish living your moments.

Ken Budd

Bob Herger

VANCOUVER

Living the Moment

BOB HERGER
&
KEN BUDD

Living the Moment

A Photographic Essay of Metro Vancouver

BOB HERGER
The Photographs

&

KEN BUDD
The Story

SummerWild

The Publisher

We Owe
A Lot
To Many

To all the wonderful
women in my life:
Megan, Carolyn, Natalie,
Stephanie, Madeline, Nyla,
and Amelia.

Bob

For all my family
and my friends
who have encouraged
my creative spirit,
and who have loved me
—especially Mom.

Ken

What's Coming Next?

The Inukshuk is a representation of the human form, marking important stops on a journey, and showing travellers that they are on the right path. This commanding sculpture on English Bay marks a very special place, an amazing community that is on the right path to succeed at the goals we have set for ourselves.

Good Deeds Will Happen Here

RICK HANSEN

Any of the distinctly unique regions of British Columbia deserve praise as some of the most beautiful places on Earth. Our province—indeed our country—is simply spectacular, abundant in culture, beauty and diversity. As I wheeled around the world on my *Man In Motion World Tour*, many of the more gruelling moments were made less painful when I let my mind drift back to my boyhood homes in some great communities in BC. Port Alberni, Fort St. John and Williams Lake will forever hold special places in my heart.

Now my work is centred in Metro Vancouver. It is where my wife and I have raised our family for the past couple of decades, nurtured by the stunning natural beauty of its rugged mountains, lush forests and seductive ocean, and especially, by its wonderful people. The outpouring of public support that flooded over my team and me as we returned to Oakridge Mall on May 22, 1987 convinced me that I might accomplish something exceptional in this place.

Since then, we have achieved outstanding progress towards making Canadian municipalities more accessible and inclusive for people with disabilities and towards finding a cure for spinal cord injury. There is, however, still a great distance to be covered on the journey we have chosen, and I believe that our best work is yet to come. It is for this reason that the constant backing from our community has been, and continues to be, so extremely important. I am deeply grateful to all those who have encouraged us along the way and whose support has enriched our purpose.

The plethora of opportunities available in this amazing community, together with the unwavering generosity of its citizens—whose backgrounds exemplify the very best of a diverse multicultural population—cause me to believe wholeheartedly that good deeds will happen here. Many already have, and more are bound to reveal themselves.

It seems only appropriate, during a time when the world's attention was focused on the 2010 Olympic and Paralympic Winter Games, that a book—in this case, a photographic essay of Metro Vancouver—should celebrate the beauty and joy we are so fortunate to experience as part of our daily lives, reminding us always to keep living the moment.

RickHansen, C.C., O.B.C.

Rick Hansen's "Man In Motion World Tour" was the impetus for the Rick Hansen Foundation, which today champions research for a cure for spinal cord injury and works to create accessible and inclusive communities for people with disabilities.

Charity of Choice: Rick Hansen Foundation
www.rickhansen.com

Living...

...Each and Every Moment

The idea was Gerry's. The genesis had been an invitation from his godparents to go sailing once spring put in an appearance, but the epiphany came while he and Natalia luxuriated in her aunt and uncle's hot tub during a dour, wet and cold late afternoon in mid-February. The routine for such visits to her relatives was always the same. They would sit down to a fabulous dinner, which inevitably was followed by a scrumptious dessert, then the obligatory after-dinner drink, and some stimulating conversation. But first and foremost, there was the usual insistence that the two young people start their visit with a soak. It was a ritual for which the newly married couple was appreciative. A look across at False Creek North through steam while being soothed by boisterous bubbles—all from atop a houseboat—was an indulgence they never refused. A good thing too, as this time it had conjured up a fun plan.

The two of them...

The two of them craved outdoor experiences. Tromping through the wet green of an ancient rainforest, drifting with a lazy current on a sunny afternoon paddle, floating skis over fresh powder, wandering a beach at sunset. These were the adventures that got their juices flowing.

Playing in the outdoors was how they met, and their mutual reverence for it was undoubtedly a major reason they fell in love. Over very little time they nurtured more sophisticated tastes together: fine dining, plays, dance recitals, concerts— even opera.

Married for not quite two years now, and just entering their thirties, they didn't feel ready to start a family. Natalia would readily admit to close friends that she and Gerry were still too young and too selfish to take such a big step, and he always agreed with her. There was too much exploring to be done, and Metro Vancouver was a perfect playground to do it in.

Both were happy they worked downtown. "Nat", Gerard's personal moniker for his new wife, was a scrub nurse at VGH. "Gerry", her not-so-French name for him, was a web designer for an up-and-coming technology business. The two

pulled down impressive salaries, with benefits to boot. Each had done a good job of tucking away substantial savings while single, scholarships staving off the need for massive student loans. They also worked a lot of evening overtime during the week, leaving the weekends for rejuvenation. Being stingy, as well, had let them stuff much of their hard-earned cash under the mattress. The resultant reward of all that fiscal frugalness was a magnificent view from their modest twelfth-floor condo on the old Expo site. Its location encouraged them to zip across False Creek on Aquabuses destined for Granville Island, to shop for fresh produce, unique dishes and to mingle with tourists. A stroll to Chinatown, just a few blocks the other side of BC and GM Places—venues where they often witnessed awesome spectacles in the form of concerts and great sports entertainment—was as much an excuse for exercise and a unique cultural experience as an opportunity to find affordable foodstuffs and household bargains.

While they got to work on foot or using transit, they had invested in a modest vehicle, flexibly designed to service their outdoor needs. It shouldered their bikes or kayaks, acted as rustic overnight accommodation, and did not break their bank on fuel and maintenance costs. The fitness centre in the condo tower added to their lean meanness, keeping them hungry to attack anything Nature threw at them. And Saturday of this coming weekend promised to present a dandy, the challenge they had planned that evening in the hot tub. Their very own Vancouver hat-trick.

Their very own Vancouver hat-trick...

The excitement brought on by anticipation made waking before dawn easier. A substantial breakfast followed a quick shower, and soon they were watching light wash over the city as they motored closer to the Lions Gate Bridge, on their way to Gleneagles Golf Club near Horseshoe Bay.

There was still little heat in the sun when they teed-off the first hole at 7:00 a.m. Nat briefly grumbled again about the idea of wasting a gorgeous morning chasing a little white ball around a park. Although comfortable with a pack on her back, or while paddling a kayak or canoe, or even swatting a tennis ball—as they often did on the numerous tennis courts scattered around the city—she didn't do well with

"...and soon they were watching light wash over the city as they motored closer to the Lions Gate Bridge, on their way to Gleneagles Golf Club near Horseshoe Bay."

other, typical sports equipment. On the other hand, while Gerry didn't have plans to play competitive golf, he did enjoy occasionally smacking a solid drive.

By the time they came to Hole #6: Apple Valley, they had given up keeping score, each not playing terribly well and both having lost a couple of balls. At least they had settled in to enjoy a superb spring morning. Unfortunately, the apple blossoms were sparse due to a recent energetic pruning, but they got to watch through a peek-a-boo view from the green as the sleek Coastal Renaissance ferry slipped into Georgia Strait on its way to Nanaimo. Gerry had secretly decided to keep the focus of the golf game on having fun, hoping that Nat would protest less about playing at it.

British Columbia was a mecca for golf enthusiasts, but there was no need to leave Metro Vancouver to enjoy a round in some of the most scenic settings anywhere. Whether it was the rolling landscapes of Furry Creek or Big Sky, two of several courses in Sea-To-Sky Country, or the popular and challenging Northview in Surrey, or historic Fraserview in Vancouver, even the keenest golfers could be sated should they commit to playing a different course each week.

Cool fire spread across it…

Eighteen holes accomplished, by noon exactly, they were relaxing with Gerry's godparents in a window of the Boathouse Restaurant on Horseshoe Bay. The Spring Shrimp Fiesta menu had served up delicious lunches, and all four were laughing their way through the dregs of a bottle of wine. His mentors had offered to host them at the West Vancouver Yacht Club where their sailboat was moored, but, being an independent devil, Gerry insisted that he and Nat treat to lunch.

Two hours later and the sailboat, Faem, with the four of them—plus canine mascot, Chlöe—was slicing through the waters past Lighthouse Park. The lighthouse was now unmanned, though still crucial to navigation, and perched as a landmark icon at the entry to English Bay. The park, with its boulder outcroppings along the shoreline, ancient rainforest, and numerous hiking trails was both a must-see for tourists and a semi-wilderness sanctuary for locals.

The extravagant homes on the West Vancouver shores were almost too opulent, though many were admittedly stunning architecturally. That observation initiated a discussion about architecture in general, and then Vancouver specifically. They all agreed that the Marine Building Downtown would deserve their award for the most enduring and endearing example of historical favourites. Hotel Vancouver, the Law Courts, and the Coliseum-like Public Library also made the short list. The recent skyscraper addition to the skyline, Shangri-La, and the legacies of Expo'86— Science World and BC Place Stadium—deserved only honourable mention. As was probably inevitable, Nat and Gerry argued about which campus deserved the most praise for its appearance; Nat was a graduate of UBC, while Gerry was an SFU alumnus.

One thing they all agreed was that it was Metro Vancouver's natural beauty and accompanying assets that labeled it one of the most spectacular metropolitan centres in the world. Gerry suggested that it was becoming a modern day version of New York, comparing Stanley Park to The Big Apple's Central Park, and noting how more and more people were choosing to live downtown, where being a slave to the automobile was less of a dictate.

Beyond the buildings, Nat believed residents should be eternally grateful for the providence their forefathers demonstrated in preserving so many greenspaces throughout the region. Not only were most communities dotted with wonderfully designed neighbourhood parks, often displaying evocative sculptures, but the geographic decree of the region resulted in scores of ravines carved by creeks, kilometers of salt and freshwater shorelines, and copses of trees spread thick to the mountaintops, all sporting signage as community, regional or provincial parks. Lighthouse, Stanley, Bear Creek, Burnaby Mountain, and Golden Ears Provincial were just a few of the amazing spots families could visit for a day's outing. And beyond these headliners were still an awesome variety and number of events— cultural, musical, artistic, athletic, environmental, and charitable—that were held in micro-communities throughout Metro Vancouver's community parks, theatres and recreation centres. Anyone who complained about a dearth of things to do in the area was likely blissfully unaware of everything from Earth Day Celebrations to the PNE, the Vancouver Symphony Orchestra to the VanDusen Garden's Plant Sale,

"Two hours later and the sailboat, Faem, with the four of them—plus canine mascot, Chlöe—was slicing through the waters..."

and aboriginal War Canoe Races at Cultus Lake to the Vancouver Marathon and the Vancouver Sun Run. Not to mention that none of these even accounted for the entertainment provided by the professional sports teams, like Canadians baseball, Whitecaps soccer, the BC Lions, the Giants or Bruins "junior" hockey teams or the beloved Vancouver Canucks.

Nat enthusiastically took over the helm of the sleek craft for a while and Gerry worried slightly that his wife might expect to own such a magnificent plaything in the future. Eventually the two settled at the bow of the boat, cuddling, and almost let the squish of the waves against the prow, the chilliness of the spring day breeze, and the brilliant sunshine—that held promise of another sensational summer—lull them to sleep. Hours later, Faem slid back into her berth at the yacht club, as the sun took to lying on the water, spreading cool fire across it.

With the darkness…

With the darkness came gorging on excellent Chinese food at Capilano Heights Chinese Restaurant. That was followed by the changing of their clothes, the grabbing of their gear, and the seemingly endless biding of time while eagerly awaiting their turn to board the gondola. Eventually they were reveling in their first run of night skiing on Grouse Mountain. It had been a great season for skiing on Grouse, so they knew ahead of time that they were going to have to contend with the reality of lineups, and that was okay with both of them. Nat was the better skier, having grown up with winters on this and other snow-capped mountain playgrounds in the area. Gerry had only tried skiing a few times while growing up in Quebec, but he had definitely taken to his new sport and was a fast learner. If he had any misgivings, it was that he had let Nat convince him that he should play in the snow on skis, instead of a snowboard.

He was enjoying himself immensely and reflected on past excursions to those other ski hills, near and far. There was a plethora of sites to choose from. While the Okanagan and Vancouver Island offered great weekend getaways, the ridge of mountains from Hope to Whistler was a haven for snow, offering up Hemlock Valley, Mount Seymour, Grouse Mountain, Cypress Mountain, and Whistler Blackcomb ski resorts. It was no wonder that Vancouver and Whistler were named hosts for the 2010 Olympic and Paralympic Winter Games.

The two skiers were exhausted after a couple of hours of crashing moguls and shooshing bowls. Having heard that it was the tired skier who most likely broke a leg taking one run too many, they decided to call it quits after this final run. Interestingly on this last glide down the slope, a couple of guys in snowshoes on the side of the run got their attention and called them over. It turned out the two were shooting photographs for a coffee table book, a photo essay on Metro Vancouver, and asked if Nat and Gerry would mind letting them take some shots for possible inclusion in their book. The book guys promised to share their folder of photographs so the two adventurers could use them on a blog or frame them for their condo wall. Nat figured it would be a great way for them to remember the unbelievable day they had just enjoyed, so they agreed.

As they were posing and grinning for the photographer, both felt ecstatic, realizing that they had achieved the goal they set for themselves in the hot tub many weeks earlier. In just a single day, they had played a full round of golf on a beautiful course in the morning, relaxed on a sailboat guided by unselfish hosts across crisp waters that afternoon, and charged down the ski slopes while the lights of a magnificent metropolis twinkled below them in the evening. A hat-trick in any hockey player's book! Where else in the world could they accomplish such a feat?

They were abundantly aware of how blessed they were to live in such an exceptional community, a beautiful province, and a richly diverse country. Neither could see living anywhere else, convinced that this city was where they would raise their family. They truly loved living each and every moment in this incredibly spectacular place that they were lucky enough to call home.

"They were abundantly aware of how blessed they were to live in such an exceptional community, a beautiful province, and a richly diverse country."

Summer

They Loved the Prairies, But...

They had both lived all their lives on the Prairies, in Saskatoon to be exact. He had enjoyed running a small accounting firm, successful enough to secure an early retirement. She had truly loved teaching Canadian history at U of S. Agreeing to start living their new lifestyle at the same time, their first order of business upon "pulling the pin" was to embark on an adventure in search of the perfect place to retire. They loved the Prairies, but both of their kids had fled to different corners of the world, so why shouldn't they embrace change?

Her contacts through teaching had yielded a condo near UBC that they could sublet from teacher friends who were off exploring Europe for the summer. Living in Metro Vancouver for a time seemed the best way for these novice retirees to decide if they wanted to spend the rest of their lives on the Coast. They believed they could substitute some of the rains of winter for Arizona sunshine—if need be.

But there was no rain to worry about now. So far, in the few weeks they had spent here, balmy weather had encouraged them to play like adventurous tourists on a first holiday. Glorious scenery, a multitude of recreational options, and wonderfully helpful and friendly people had proven exciting constants.

A week earlier they spent the day wandering around the UBC campus, investing most of their time intoxicated by the artifacts in the Museum of Anthropology. A transit bus provided access there, and they hoped they could utilize the same kind of transportation when they took in SFU in a few days. They did have to take the car to the Fort Langley Historic Site, but that worked out to their advantage. She was so taken with the historical significance of the Fraser Valley, they ended up staying in a local B&B overlooking the mighty river, and spent the next day getting acquainted with local fruit wineries and the outlying communities of Maple Ridge, Mission, and Abbotsford. They had crossed over the river via the new Golden Ears Bridge, and the loop drive they chose permitted them to pick their own blueberries at Aldergrove on the way home. She accused him playfully of putting more in his mouth than in the basket.

The parks and points of interest were so numerous they instinctively knew that retirement here would involve activity. They had fish and chips on the dock at Steveston, and laughed when a seagull swiped a French fry off her plate. That lunch was followed by a fascinating tour of the old cannery.

A day later, and this time they picnicked on a rocky bluff beside the lighthouse at Lighthouse Park, with the city of Vancouver an enticing gemstone across the bay in the distance. Then there was the cool, evocatively ancient walk through the old growth forest back to their vehicle.

Dinner atop Grouse Mountain was memorable, as was watching the grizzly bears and the bird show earlier in the day. The couple had been distracted from their study of the animals by paragliders soaring overhead. The two loved hiking, and wondered, as they looked out at the adjoining mountain peaks, if they were up to making it to the summit of The Lions, those two impressive peaks visible from almost anywhere in Downtown Vancouver.

Today had been Stanley Park's turn. The husband and wife team had meandered through innumerable forest trails and even taken a swim in the outdoor pool. The sights of Canada Place and the Convention Centre from the cluster of totem poles, the North Shore Mountains from the Nine O'Clock Gun, and Lions Gate Bridge from Lumberman's Arch were downright energizing. And then there were the several hours they allotted to investigating all the impressive exhibits the Vancouver Aquarium offered. A delicious seafood dinner at the Fish House ended their exploring and seemed a perfect precursor to a finishing walk on the Seawall at sunset. They knew they would be fascinated there by the different kinds of people—many with lovable dogs—and the curious blend of smells, a mixture of sunblocks, exotic perfumes, and appetizing aromas wafting from curbside food stalls. A young street musician plucking his guitar set the perfect ambience.

What to do tomorrow? Shopping on Robson Street? Watching the volleyball enthusiasts compete at Kitsilano or the sailboats slip across the bay while wandering the Spanish Banks? Were they still young enough at heart to try sunbathing in the nude on Wreck Beach?

Patriotism has little to do with ethnicity, and much more with generational values. Wearing the colours, waving the flag, and wistfully watching the Canada Day Parade with wonder sets an example for our children, and instills in them the importance of belonging to a nation that is simply the best.

The former site of the World Exposition in 1986 has now been developed into a major residential centre of impressive skyscrapers on the north shore of False Creek. The waterway is a traffic artery for all sorts of watercraft, including sturdy little Aquabuses.

A metropolis partially surrounded by water demands different forms of transportation to move a significant number of bodies across various creeks, rivers, inlets, and even a strait. BC Ferries handles travel to and from Vancouver Island, the Gulf Islands and the Sunshine Coast via the Horseshoe Bay and Tsawwassen terminals, while the trusty SeaBus shuttles passengers between Downtown Vancouver and the North Shore.

Scullers worship water that could be mistaken for glass, and Coal Harbour does not often disappoint. One benefit of training on this "glass" is the opportunity to admire the waterborne transportation hub centred around the sweeping sails of Canada Place, an unmistakable landmark.

In valleys, on and beside lakes and streams, and up into the mountains, in alpine meadows and on craggy ledges, hiking the high country is a recreation appreciated by more than just fanatics. Vast numbers of outdoor enthusiasts take the easy way up by using the lifts on Whistler and Blackcomb, as others tackle backbreaking journeys on foot to Black Tusk and Garibaldi Lake, or even into complete wilderness beyond. Success reveals fields of flowers to photograph and wildlife to be studied.

Perched on its peak and flanked by The Lions, Grouse Mountain Resort invites its local neighbours below and visitors from around the world to participate in an assortment of entertaining activities. Among the opportunities for fun, grizzly bears—which can be found in the wild beyond Whistler—named Coola and Grinder headline the Refuge for Endangered Wildlife. Meanwhile eagles, hawks and falcons captivate crowds at the "Birds in Motion" demonstration. Thrill seekers attempt flight of their own by paragliding from the peak, and everyone marvels at the skill demonstrated in the lumberjack shows.

A Magnet for All

A bounty of retail outlets, artist studios and light industry, providing an almost infinite number and variety of products, is crammed into 37 acres of unique real estate in the heart of Metro Vancouver. Today's Granville Island was reincarnated from an industrial site in the late 1970s. Offering fresh organic produce, meats, seafood, candy, bakery goods, and much more, the Public Market is the epicenter of this reconstituted shopping mecca. Complementing it on the island are eateries, gift shops, a bookstore, a hotel, art galleries and one-of-a-kind businesses. Then there is the marina, the houseboat colony, and the renowned Emily Carr University of Art and Design, where the grace of traditional fine art meets the future in graphic and industrial design. In the evenings theatre-goers are spoiled for choice, with several performance venues dotting the island. All tucked for the most part under a bridge, millions of tourists and locals flock here each year.

*While another day of summer beach activity fades, a lone fitness keener satisfies an inner mandate
by enjoying a solitary swim at Kits Pool. Outdoor pools throughout the region complement numerous
indoor pools, creeks, rivers, lakes and the Pacific Ocean—all frequented by water-lovers.*

The spectacle of Science World—a legacy of Expo '86 now known as the Telus World of Science—draws masses each year, especially groups of eager school students. Just after sunset, it can, after all these years, still look futuristic.

Commonly referred to as The Planetarium, the H.R. MacMillan Space Centre is also a Vancouver landmark, offering a multitude of programs relating to the heavens. With its Star Theatre and Cosmic Courtyard, the centre demystifies the final frontier.

Beginning in childhood, sand is a field of play. It starts with building sandcastles or simply grinding it between the toes. Like anywhere, fun in the sand on any of Metro Vancouver's many beaches is a favourite summer pastime. On Boundary Bay, endless tidal flats permit "squatters" to create an umbrella shelter.

As we "mature", sand often becomes a real playing field. Throughout the summer, at several locations on the city's beaches, volleyball is the lure for games in the sand. Matches can be between a group of friends or strangers who organize a pick-up game, or can be contests of a more serious nature. Competitive beach volleyball is gaining in popularity, with teams contending in organized leagues on courts popping up all over Metro Vancouver.

With the summer sun beaming down on popular beaches nearer downtown, sunbathers escape the rush of a busy city. On a less manicured beach, a couple of would-be fisherwomen dip their nets into riffles made by gentle waves, hoping to catch a unique specimen from the sea.

Riders from the Cove Bike Factory Racing Team show off at Whistler's Crankworx Festival.

Wheels on different racing bikes churn toward the finish line at the annual Tour de Gastown.

Sports that are idolized in many parts of the world are also favourites here

Vancouver Whitecaps FC has an extensive youth soccer program, a W-League women's side, and a first-rate men's team. With a couple of USL Playoff Championships under their belt, the men are worthy of their recent promotion to MLS—the highest level of soccer in North America.

Cricket is played and watched every weekend in Stanley Park by a greater number of followers than imagined.

On a mountain slope or in a sheltered bay, there is always a place or way to play. The corridor along the Sea-To-Sky Highway to Whistler and beyond is just one of the playgrounds for golfers in the region. With its superb views, Furry Creek, as well as Nicklaus North and Big Mountain—to name just a few—are undeniably appealing. There are dozens more courses speckling Metro Vancouver to thrill the "golf nut".

On English Bay, Howe Sound or Georgia Strait, sailors of all sizes of boats cause their crafts to slice through inviting waters. The many participants in the Easter Seals Waves Regatta pray for wind to drive them forward. Through generous corporate donations, the regatta raises nearly a quarter-million dollars annually in support of Easter Seals House, and even during the thick of the race, there is still time to hang out—or hang over.

Facing one of the great trials Nature has to offer, intrepid souls flock to the Chief and other rock challenges near Squamish. The Chief is known as one of the foremost granite monoliths in North America, and is loved particularly by crack climbers. Self-actualization creates downright giddiness among climbing sisters after topping out.

The Drop Zone is equal parts frighteningly horrific and exhilaratingly enlightening. Whether it is legitimate altruism or the need for an awesome adrenalin rush, hanging in space to raise money for the BC Lions Society for Children with Disabilities is not for the faint-of-heart. Comic book heroes step up—or hang out!

The bliss of yoga, ever more popular in community and fitness centres, is experienced in its purest and most peaceful form when practicing in natural surroundings. Tranquil "Yogis" are a common sight for seaside walkers at serene Sunset Beach.

Strolling along the Seawall at Third Beach, early evening wanderers marvel at the balancing act of an itinerant sculptor whose skills create performance art.

Shorelines make great playgrounds. The rock outcroppings of West Vancouver's Lighthouse Park, right through to Horseshoe Bay, are classics. They are forever special places where generations of buddies can gather for a late afternoon swim. And, not only are they incredible perches for magnificent homes, like those in Eagle Harbour, they are also havens for serious sailors.

Around the corner, any day of the year, Whytecliff Park hosts avid SCUBA divers, who marvel at the undersea world's unique wildlife, such as vibrant sea stars. On weekends especially, the park is like a sea lion rookery, attracting many divers.

The first ball was thrown out at Nat Bailey Stadium in 1951. In perhaps the prettiest little ballpark in North America, our boys of summer, the Vancouver Canadians, ply their trade here, vying for their ticket to "the show"—a spot on a major league baseball team. Fans enjoy a great game, and the atmosphere, a hot dog, and a cold beer (for big kids only) are always winners.

Across the way, colours abound, and there is sweetness in the air. An industry of the past has today become a place of beauty. The Quarry, a significant sanctuary within Queen Elizabeth Park, seduces visitors as they wander the grounds and feel their stress slip away.

Those lazy, hazy, crazy days of summer! For youngsters, there is nothing more idyllic to do on a hot summer day than to add a bit of danger to adventure by dangling over a log that spans Kanaka Creek in Maple Ridge.

For adults, floating on inner tubes down Gold Creek or Lynn Creek—or any other in the region—and feeling as though you are bobbing along on liquid emerald is the perfect way to while away a sunny afternoon.

Creeks carve ravines and canyons, and while many can be dangerous to explore, tourists and locals alike get to marvel at Nature's power by crossing the more spectacular abysses on suspension bridges, such as the one at Lynn Canyon Park and the famous Capilano Suspension Bridge.

Our Jewel Shines

Considered the crown jewel of the city, Stanley Park—a mainstay of Vancouver life since 1887—welcomes any and all to meander its winding, forested paths and to walk its Seawall. Home to majestically swaying cedar, hemlock and fir trees, all humbling in size, this unparalleled piece of temperate rainforest has survived early logging and hurricane-force windstorms, and is now a protected reserve visited by millions each year. The Vancouver Aquarium is a must-see, as is the impressive collection of First Nations totems from the coastal regions of British Columbia. Then there are performances to be enjoyed at Theatre Under the Stars, The Rose Garden to be in awe of, and horse-drawn carriages to be romanced by. Smiles and laughter fill the park in summer as kids splash in the water park or climb aboard the Miniature Train. More transient visitors pass through—or around—the park via its Seawall, a paved passageway celebrated by those travelling on foot or wheels, which skirts the seaside circumference of the park. Some of the best views are taken in from this path's entrance at Coal Harbour, home to the Vancouver Rowing Club.

The West End of Vancouver is the epicentre of two major celebrations each summer.

For three decades, the Pride Parade has been the culmination of a series of events that celebrate inclusion and herald a unique spirit and culture. The outlandish costumes and sometimes-bizarre antics attract not only residents of Vancouver's West End, but people from all over Metro Vancouver and from outside the region.

The HSBC Celebration of Light is a much-anticipated summer event for hundreds of thousands of onlookers. As teams compete for the title, fireworks fanatics compete for the best vantage point, swarming the beaches and high-rise rooftops surrounding English Bay. Many others bob in boats offshore. The pyro-musical display pits countries against each other to create the most outstanding extravaganza, each presenting on a different night, with a collective grand finale to follow. The spectacle is spread over a couple of weeks, encouraging spectators to return again and again.

The Fraser Valley is a willing host to those who love to take to the air. Conceived in 1962, the annual Abbotsford International Air Show attracts a hundred thousand flight enthusiasts over the three-day weekend event. Most would be thrilled to pilot or at least sit in the cockpit of a B-25 Mitchell or a P-51 Thunder Mustang, such as the two flying in formation over The Abbey, just outside Mission.

The Vancouver Soaring Association has its home—or its airbase— in Chilliwack. Members soar between mountain peaks and over communities, such as Hope, held aloft by thermal updrafts. The gliders sometimes carry lucky, awestruck passengers.

Given the right atmospheric conditions, a ride in a hot air balloon floats participants from the take-off location in Langley, over lush farm fields, rural homesteads, rivers and lakes, and past the Northview Golf and Country Club, designed by Arnold Palmer.

In perfect contradiction, a monstrous cruise ship can maneuver under Lions Gate Bridge on its journey to Alaska, as a solitary fisherman wishes for the strike of a wayward salmon when he throws in his line off the mouth of the Capilano River.

Continuing its journey, the ship, carrying a couple thousand passengers, shares the waters of English Bay with far more diminutive watercraft.

The cruise ship industry is significant for the Port of Vancouver and many other businesses. Almost a million passengers from all over the globe board more than 250 sailings each year to cruise the Inside Passage as a special vacation.

Cornucopia

Sticking to the "100-Mile Diet" is as easily done as said in the Fraser Valley. Savory samples of every food group can be dug-up, picked, plucked, tapped and gathered from this fertile region.

Delicious honey is collected from hives placed amongst magenta fireweed flowers in the logged-off areas of mountain slopes above Chilliwack. Sweet and spicy peppers are nurtured in hot houses in South Delta, while a Ladner farmer makes sure there are spuds for the pot, and willing workers harvest celery in Burnaby.

Bizarre microclimates also allow for more exotic foodstuffs to be grown, much to the delight of local restaurateurs, who lean toward locally-grown ingredients. Generally mild weather ensures that the Valley's spoils can be enjoyed year-round. Farm fields—and much more—feed us!

Should they crave a more intimate space, young lovers can easily leave the push of Robson Street for the more peaceful environs of somewhere like Vanier Park, or they could ramp up the energy and head to the PNE—unconcerned about finding a parking spot in either situation.

The Pacific National Exhibition, a traditional way to say goodbye to summer holidays and hello to the new school year, has a lot to offer. There are the rides, the food, and the special events and activities. A day at the PNE is an annual pilgrimage for many living here, who eagerly look forward to being jostled by the throng or being "gastronomically challenged" when upside-down and out-of-control on an insane ride.

Viewed from Lumbermen's Arch along the Seawall, there is no denying the prominence of Lions Gate Bridge's distinct, iconic status. Built in 1937 as a way to develop the North Shore, and renovated in the late 1990s, it is one of the area's traffic lifelines.

The perfect way to say goodbye to a beautiful summer day is to bask in the alpenglow of sunset while walking the Seawall around Siwash Rock.

It is a given that Canadians are hockey crazy, but a group of the craziest—unable to wait for the Canucks

to take to the ice again in the fall—create a different kind of rink at Spanish Banks, and get to shout,

"He shoots! He scores!" in mid-summer.

I Love This City

BILL GOOD

It's a good idea when you look around sometimes to remember where we came from. I've always loved this city. My folks came here from Winnipeg when I was very little. I now have no memory of Manitoba, but have vivid memories of Vancouver.

When I look around today it's hard to believe that within my lifetime we have developed from a relatively small city, made up mostly of people with European roots, to a metropolis with a hugely diverse population comprised of people from all over the world. I relish the fact that you can have Arabs and Jews, Hindus, Sikhs, and Muslims, all living and working together—and all cheering for, or playfully arguing about, the Canucks.

I was at a hockey game recently, awed by eye-popping video on that mammoth screen, and I reflected back to my first experience with the Western League Canucks, as a twelve year old boy, in the old PNE Forum. What a difference. I grew up going to BC Lions games in what was a brand new Empire Stadium. It's almost unimaginable that its replacement, state-of-the-art BC Place, is now in need of refurbishing.

The world came to Expo '86 and many stayed. That was the start of the marvelous transformation of False Creek, Yaletown, and Coal Harbour. Walk around the Westin Bayshore toward the new convention centre, past the marina. Remarkable. The last time I did that I pinched myself and said, "We really live here?" Prudent planners also created Granville Island Market, a pretty unique shopping experience at the time.

In twenty-five years, instead of becoming congested and unlivable, good planning has created a city that people want to live and work in. Fewer people commute into Vancouver today than a decade ago, as many of us have chosen to move downtown and avoid the long limp home.

Nothing stays the same forever, but Stanley Park seems a constant. The park is a jewel at the heart of this magnificent city. If you take the time to walk the Seawall, or even just cruise the park drive, it's a reminder of how those who came before us got a lot of things right.

I've been talking primarily about Vancouver, but think, too, about all that's available to us without having to go far, whether in greater Metro Vancouver or up the Sea-To-Sky Highway. People travel across the globe to ski and snowboard at Whistler Blackcomb. We can hit the slopes in a couple of hours.

My wife, Georgy, and I have been blessed by the opportunity to travel to about fifty other countries. We've seen a lot of great places, but none that could tempt us to leave this place. Even in our home away from home on the Sunshine Coast, we are never really far away, and I am comforted by the warm glow of the city's lights and the familiar sight of UBC across the inlet. I've always loved this city.

Bill Good

Bill Good

Bill Good hosts his own show on CKNW Radio and is co-anchor of CTV/BC News. Between Bill and his late father, Bill Sr., there's been a Good on radio and TV in BC for sixty years.

Charity of choice: CKNW Orphan's Fund
www.cknw.com

Autumn

Run of the River

The paddle bit into the water. Its gurglings, the only sounds in the gray dawn, were affirmations of the serenity surrounding him, of the progress he was making, and of his decision to slip out of bed to commune with Nature before Megan and the kids awoke. Behind him the first light of day was desperately trying to permeate the glut of fog that pervaded everything along the bank. Sunrise on Alouette River seemed designed for his pleasure.

His shoulders and neck no longer screamed of the pain brought on by the portage from his canoe's travel cradle atop the car to the river's edge. The canoe, an old friend left to him by his father and his grandfather before him, showed little sign of wear. His loving maintenance of the trusty craft made sure that it ably matched his new hybrid vehicle in stature. He was pleased that his actions to preserve his special world spoke louder than words.

The morning was an example of his favourite time of day and year. His steady rhythm with the paddle staved off the chill in the air, although icy splashes on his hands caused his fingers to ache. Deep breaths sucked moisture from the mist. The muscles in his back and arms delighted in the strain, encouraging this weekly ritual. Already a Great Blue Heron had clattered from a patch of reeds to his right, its emergence from the white blanket causing swirls that settled into a rose-coloured gauze. A small flush of Mallards broke from the same cover and took flight just a few hundred meters beyond. The tiny flock lifted over glorious gold and red leaves that adorned the maple trees bordering the waterway, quacking displeasure at being chased away. The dew-damp leaves were now catching a few boisterous rays of light and glittering like jewels. All were surprises that caused his heart to beat faster.

Everything in his life was in sync: a thriving family, a comfortable home away from the buzz of city congestion, and a balance between his challenging work and a recreational lifestyle that could be enjoyed in places like this. He closed his brain from the reality that in a couple of hours he would be boarding the West Coast Express for his morning commute to his downtown office. At least the train ride gave him the choice of reading, prepping for his workday, or just getting lost in the scenery as it flashed by.

A coyote yipped from behind some brush along the riverbank. He couldn't see it, but knew it was close, and wondered whether it was this year's pup. Was it calling its mother, baffled by how it was now so alone? Or was it jubilant because it had pounced on an unsuspecting vole, a morning snack? He loved Nature's mysteries.

He kept labouring, the river's push making his effort easier.

Rounding a protruding mound, he was astounded once again by the view of the jagged peaks, a backdrop for Golden Ears Provincial Park. The tall spires jutted above the smooth pink run of the river and the amorphous layer of cotton, like determined guardians protecting Nature's fragility. This vista marked his turning-back point. A glimpse of its spectacular beauty could sustain him for days. If the weather permitted, he would cajole Megan into sharing a longer adventure this weekend—with the kids in tow.

He reefed back on the paddle to initiate a rotation that would head him in the opposite direction, and realized he was smiling at the ease of his expertise. Then he dug in, deciding to sprint against the lazy current to test his true resolve, and started back. An animal splashed in bulrushes to his left. The pungent smell of vegetation turning back into nutrients stuffed his nostrils. Birdsong had begun to fill the air. And sunlit beams almost blinded him as they sliced through what was now only a haze.

He headed home. If he had planned it right, he would get to wake Kate and Zack for school, the joy of which he never tired. He would shower quickly, and then concoct a batch of his famous banana and blueberry pancakes. Even Megan couldn't resist them.

Life was good. But then again, why shouldn't it be? After all, it was autumn in the Fraser Valley.

It's not the Cat in the Hat, but a hunter in the back acreage. Where old farm machinery becomes an art piece, and the garden is either a profusion of colour or an overgrowth of early autumnal blooms, a pet stalks a possible snack.

In an apple orchard, also somewhere in the Fraser Valley, a Bantam rooster and his brood of hens might consider keeping an eye out for intruders. The fowl could attract a coyote, a weasel or a skunk, and the apples, if not soon picked and put in the larder, could end up food for a not-so-itinerant black bear–which could have a day-bed in the copse of alders and vine maples out back.

Rapture

Like a mythological, divine spirit, a member of Vancouver's iconic music company communes with Nature while practicing her art in the ancient rainforest of Lighthouse Park in West Vancouver.

The Vancouver Symphony Orchestra has prevailed since 1919, and has claimed the majestic Orpheum Theatre as its home since the late seventies. It also presents concerts at various venues throughout Metro Vancouver, as well as the alpine meadows of Whistler Mountain. The Orpheum opened its doors in 1927 as a vaudeville theatre, and then became the grandame of movie theatres until 1974, when it enjoyed a major facelift.

As a complement to the music culture and a harmonious counterpoint to the VSO, Ballet BC offers the beauty and grace of dance. Opera and live theatre also flourish in Metro Vancouver.

A seiner heads into Georgia Strait to northern fishing grounds, while indifferent trumpeter swans look for a food source. Leaving from the same Steveston base, another fish boat departs, but this time with the full moon rising behind Mt. Baker to guide it on its way.

Constructed in 1894, the Imperial Cannery—now known as the Gulf of Georgia Cannery—was at one time the largest fish processing facility in the British Commonwealth. Today it still moors more fishing boats than any other port in Canada.

Tromping along the pier at White Rock, a father and son fishing team call it quits for the evening. For another family, the honey light of sunset is the perfect time to appreciate a gorgeous Georgia Strait vista, as they walk and wheel along the dyke in Richmond.

Vancouver is closing in on New York as far as downtown livability. False Creek North is an example of making maximum use of vertical living space, with opulent high rises perpetually springing up from the old Expo '86 site, and with a lengthy waterfront walkway that is part of a planned trail linking UBC to SFU.

SkyTrain is just one of the rapid transit systems in Metro Vancouver. Newer lines link Richmond with Downtown Vancouver, and Coquitlam with Commercial Drive. The original line runs along the Fraser River to Surrey, passing through New Westminster, the community that not only boasts being the first major settlement of this now metropolis, but also hails as the province's original capital.

The Coliseum-like Vancouver Public Library is a beautiful addition and wonderful resource to the downtown core. Its vaulted atrium is lined with shops and cafés, reminiscent of a European piazza.

Fort Langley is a National Historic Site. The original fort, a significant fur trading post for the Hudson's Bay Company over a century and a half ago, has been handsomely restored. Its prime location on the banks of the mighty Fraser River and its proximity to the First Nations of the West Coast ensured its future value.

Today, visitors will not only hear about the lifestyle of that past era from interpreters dressed in period clothing, but will also take part in activities that were prevalent then, such as barrel-making and panning for gold. Afterward, a walk to Derby Reach along the Fort-to-Fort Trail combines nature, history and culture.

During this exploration of the past, a reminder of the present may chug by on the river. A stout tug pulls a log boom to the nearest sawmill—with the omnipresent Mt. Baker overlooking.

Autumn leaves crunch underfoot as a little tyke, having morphed into a butterfly, fantasizes the life of such a creature while she flits and flutters down a Richmond street.

Were she to trick-or-treat in Ladner, she might come across a family of jack-o'-lanterns waiting to offer her a Hallowe'en apple.

Harvesting Riches

A plentiful yield is realized each fall season, be it walnuts from a grove in appropriately-named Walnut Grove or cranberries from a bog in Pitt Meadows. Whether they shake and rake or wet-pick, growers around Metro Vancouver have their own distinct ways of bringing Nature's delights to our pantries. Many harvests are marked by unique community festivals that celebrate the reaping of local rewards.

In Langley, Alsace-inspired viticulture has helped etch out a place in the catalogue of the world's wine-producing regions. Named after the Roman God of wine, Bacchus grapes are left to grow plump and ripen. Just before the fall harvest, entire vineyards are covered with giant netting to keep avian invaders at bay. A more frequent produce, dairy farmers from throughout the Fraser Valley offer up fresh milk to refrigerators daily.

A fly-fisherwoman deftly casts her line into Pitt River on a frosty autumn morning.

Another gal walks her faithful steed on a Campbell Valley Park equestrian trail in Langley.

These days, recreation takes on countless forms, according to personal taste. Some seek productive pursuits in the outdoors. Others prefer indoors, "huge" indoors.

When the BC Lions are performing at their most competitive, which is generally always, fans fill BC Place, shouting their praise in support of a winning team.

The massive dome is also home to trade shows, such as the Vancouver International Boat Show, the Home and Garden Show, the Outdoor and Golf & Travel Shows, and Monster Jam.

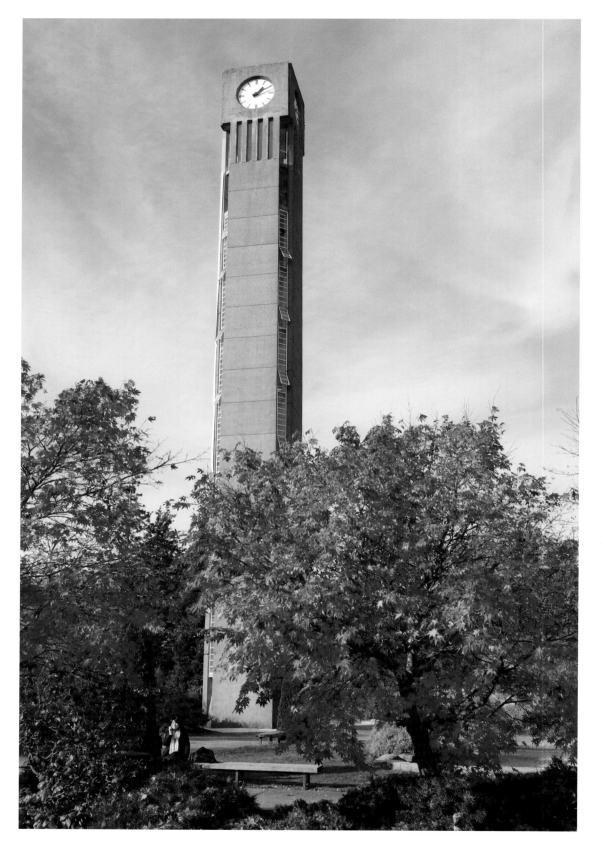

Loving Learning

Our youth are undoubtedly our most precious resource. Consistent with the knowledge that educated youth will be better equipped to meet the challenges of tomorrow and to keep our country a global leader, there are almost 300,000 students in Metro Vancouver's K-12 public education system—half of all students in the province.

For higher learning, there are no less than six public universities, two public technical institutes, and three public colleges, offering up every program under the sun. The three major institutions of UBC, SFU and BCIT account for an additional 100,000 full and part-time students alone.

Add to all of this an ever-increasing population of international students from Europe, Asia, and Latin America, who attend hundreds of language and career colleges, and it becomes very clear that education is big business in Metro Vancouver.

Scores of people are drawn to Nitobe Garden in springtime to welcome new blooms. Yet many remain unacquainted with the sheer beauty of one of Vancouver's most gorgeous places during autumn's warm summer afterthought.

Whenever the stress of everyday life seems ready to overwhelm, wander to the local park, where a solitary but welcoming bench, like one on Alma in the Point Grey area of Vancouver, undoubtedly awaits.

If non-golfers could just once experience the bliss that comes from wandering through a manicured "park"

in the early dawn hours, they too would become devotees of the game. The Meadow Gardens Golf Club

in Pitt Meadows is just one of many such parks.

Under a Fallen Leaf

SQUIRE BARNES

In Vancouver, the four seasons never arrive at their appointed times. This delay is cursed in the early days of spring and summer, but it is happily accepted in autumn. It seems that during the first weeks of fall, only the leaves truly understand the time of year. They alter their color and take their death plunge from the trees. However, the sun never appears to be in any hurry to head south, and the mountains haven't nearly begun to paint themselves white. Autumn in Vancouver is summer's encore. Why leave the building when the crowd is yelling for more?

This double dose of summer leads Vancouverites to wonder why every Canadian doesn't live here. Outside of a love of wheat, or a fear of mountains, what is the point, really, of spending your life on the Prairies? Then there's the east of the country, where autumn is in constant danger of being kidnapped by winter, and held for days on end. Sure, it rains a lot in the final month of a Vancouver autumn, but has anyone ever had to shovel rain?

If you want a true appreciation for our summer-like fall, talk to a golfer. These are people who morbidly revel in dreadful weather reports from other parts of Canada, while driving to their local course to smack one down the fairway. Granted, a fallen leaf occasionally conceals a ball during an autumnal outing, but does that matter when your cousin from Toronto can't even pull his clubs out of storage until mid-April? Hardly. The mere fact that you can play golf, or tennis, or walk outside without a survival suit at this time of year is what separates Vancouver from most of Canada.

One birthright afforded only to Vancouverites is the right to complain about the rain. Our rain. You see, if you're from Vancouver and it's raining for days on end, you can voice your displeasure, even in a public forum. But, if you're not from Vancouver, and you show contempt for wet days, especially in public, you will quickly be put on the next plane home. No going back to the hotel to pack, no goodbyes to your friends and relatives. Just gone. You see, we are a proud yet insecure people.

For all its uniqueness, though, Vancouver is no country within a country. Like Canadians from sea to sea, we are followers of Canada's unofficial religion: Hockey. In Vancouver, the main shrine is GM Place, home of the Canucks. Idol worship is encouraged there, and idols are sold as action figures and bobbleheads at souvenir shops, where these deities can be both praised and ridiculed—depending on what they've done lately. Voice your displeasure, say what you want, there is no such thing as blasphemy. With 18,000 revellers packed into this church at a time, and scores more watching on TV, belief in the Nirvana of a successful season is at its highest point during the fall. Sadly, not very often has the belief in hockey heaven continued through to winter and spring, as too often the prophets are proven false by the time winter takes hold.

Autumn is supposed to be a kind of slow death before winter. But it doesn't quite work that way in Vancouver. Instead the city offers up all its gifts at once. Invite your friends and relatives from out of town so they can experience this unique phenomenon. Just be sure to remind them, that if they moan about the rain, they're going home early.

Squire Barnes

Born and raised in Burnaby, Squire Barnes is a homegrown sportscaster, writer, and producer, and a part of the Global TV family since 1992. He has written, produced, or performed in every medium.

Charity of choice: BC Children's Hospital
www.bcchildrens.ca

Winter

Bucking Each Mogul

Crashing down the slopes, bucking each mogul with their boards, they were thriving on the cold, fresh powder, and mountain beauty. The incredible view over the city below was almost taken for granted. Fueled by the adrenalin rush, they were giddy to carve until the inner workings of their knees felt about to shatter. Mount Seymour was their home playing field, and they knew each twist, turn, drop, and cut better than they knew their backyards. In winter, this was their backyard, and today had been outstanding. The weather gods had conjured up an eclectic mix of snow, light rain, dense fog and then brilliant sunshine, all in only a few hours. Nothing could smell cleaner. No experience could be more pure.

They were two good buddies, young guys into fun, fitness and feminine forms. Part-time jobs at the Cove Bike Shop and affluent parents who were willing to subsidize their love of adventure—as long as they stayed out of trouble—sustained them financially. High school was still a necessity, and they were both capable students, but these lads weren't about joining school teams. They couldn't wait to start university, where they could build timetables that permitted them long weekends on the local mountains—or maybe on the Island or in the Interior. The two were determined to get the most out of life, and that meant communing almost daily with Nature's creations. Like every citizen of Metro Vancouver, they realized how this superb area conjured up every outdoor challenge imaginable.

It was truly an effort just to keep up with what the North Shore Mountains offered each season. Winter was their favourite. This weekend they were playing with their old friend, a ski hill that had continued to grow as they did. Last weekend, though, it was up to Cypress Mountain and the specialty areas created for boarders as part of the Games. Then there was Grouse, and the opportunity to meet novice young females, who lapped up the attention of two good-looking expert boarders, keen to help out with free lessons. Night skiing added a romantic bonus to an already loved pursuit.

One of their greatest pursuits was a chance for the odd weekend in Whistler, a place where each arrival had them believing they had once again discovered Utopia. A multitude of varied and outstanding runs, incredible snow conditions on both Whistler and Blackcomb Mountains, and a nightlife that had them drooling with expectation all drew them magnetically. The whole scene made them wish they could skip right through the next phase of their schooling to become full-time ski bums—or maybe "board bums" more appropriately. Their visions of their futures included living at Whistler, attacking the slopes all day and partying all night. Of course, their parents had a different plan.

Snowboarding was their life until the ski hills shut down for the summer. The much-touted, world-class resort area possessed a magic formula that drew millions of visitors from around the globe, not just for the skiing and the 2010 Winter Games, but for year round recreation. With the snow gone, their snowboards gave way to their mountain bikes, which they hoisted onto racks for major overhauls at the start of every bike season. Keeping their bikes and their own bodies fit needed to be an obsession if they wanted to join the Cove Bike Shop's Factory Racing Team. That's why they invested in a new pair of lug-soled runners each spring, so they could train by tackling the Grouse Grind once a week. Their regimen for honing their fantastic physiques also included weekly runs—not hikes—along parts of the Baden-Powell Trail, a well-trodden path that follows the spine of the North Shore Mountains from Horseshoe Bay to Deep Cove, and on. It is a trip to marvel at, and the extreme heights invite them to think about getting into mountain climbing, perhaps starting with an indoor wall and then eventually braving The Chief at Squamish.

For now, though, enough light was left to bomb down several more runs, and there were still lots of ski bunnies on the hill to meet. Each wait in the chair lineup gave them an opportunity to enjoy a new scent or chat up a potential new friend. And each experience was confirmation that they enjoyed the greatest lifestyle on Earth.

The pink blush of early evening gives the Vancouver skyline a distinct ethereal quality, while the snow-capped peaks invite winter activity lovers to partake.

A little sweetie glides or "stutter-steps" on skates for the first time atop Grouse Mountain.

The festive season of winter, while celebrated by different cultures and religions in diverse ways, is always a time for us to show how much we care about each other—with more than commercial gifts, hopefully.

Boats, having donned colourful Christmas lights, wait at anchor by Granville Island Marina for the call to join the procession in the annual Carol Ships Parade of Lights.

Despite burdensome responsibilities, it is hard to keep an avid golfer down.

So much for denying that cold water affects the body. This trio proves that when H_2O is close to freezing, a person can actually turn blue!

Some people will do anything for attention! Determined to have good fun, despite the bone-chilling jolt to every aspect of one's being, a clutch of brave souls retreats from the freezing waters of English Bay following the Polar Bear Swim, which takes place every New Year's Day.

It could be to escape the summer heat, but it's often a way to avoid becoming drenched by winter downpours. Whatever the instigation, a day at the Vancouver Aquarium is an exceptional investment in learning and fun, where those of all ages will be wonderstruck by undersea marvels.

A mantle of snow can create the perfect picture postcard, such as that of Meadow Gardens Golf Club in Pitt Meadows, which can often be covered by a blanket of white. Rain will soon wash the frosting away, and that will entice golfers to swing again—even in the middle of winter.

Cross-country skiing also provides opportunities to enjoy magnificent mountain vistas. The extensive network of long and varied trails in Callaghan Valley and at Whistler Olympic Park will satisfy even the most ardent athlete.

A Winter Paradise

Touted for years as home to the best ski resort in the world, Whistler is much more than a major site of the 2010 Olympic and Paralympic Winter Games.

It has long been a preferred vacation destination for skiers and boarders from around the globe, and a walk along the Village Stroll on any day could reveal a dozen different languages being spoken. With its charming and architecturally stunning village centre and exciting night life to accent the mountain experience, thousands upon thousands come to challenge the runs that spread across the faces of Whistler and Blackcomb, now connected by the intrepid Peak 2 Peak gondola ride.

For those afraid of heights, there is no shortage of other winter sports on offer, including snowshoeing, snowmobiling, and dog sledding.

Then, in the summer…

It begins with gliding on a pair of weird shoes with blades, and then speed of movement encourages a feeling of effortless joy. That evolves to a stick and a flattened ball of hard rubber, and a game with rules, which also requires tenacity and strength and assertiveness. Ultimately, it most likely fades into a dream unfulfilled, yet there is always the thrill of watching those who master the game's demands and who get to play it at the highest level.

The Vancouver Canucks make fans rabid with enthusiasm as they attempt to will their beloved team to the greatest of hockey prizes, The Stanley Cup. GM Place erupts with shouts of "Go Canucks Go" and tens of thousands are glued to the television mouthing the same whenever our warriors step onto the ice of their home arena.

Typically drawing bigger crowds than the city's New Year's Eve festivities, celebrations for Chinese New Year—marking the start of the lunar calendar—engulf the streets and walkways of Vancouver's Chinatown in early February. A sundry of entertainment, food, culture and art provides something for all ages, and myth comes to life as children playfully accept roles of the hunter and the hunted.

Later, gracefully precise movements capture the attention and the eye as dancers float along spectator-lined streets in the enchanting parade organized by the Chinese Benevolent Association. Shops along the route ornament themselves in art comprised of vibrant colours with a "Raincity" twist.

Raptor Rookery

Just north of Squamish, at Brackendale Eagles Provincial Park, an annual phenomenon occurs between mid-November and mid-February. An average of two thousand bald eagles, most arriving from late December to mid-January, descend along the Cheakamus River Valley to gorge on the leavings of the chum salmon run. These emblematic birds of prey become more sociable in winter during migration, and large groups may gather to roost in a single tree. Even unseen, their distinct—sometimes haunting—cries are as staggering as their larger-than-life presence. It is one of the largest gatherings of bald eagles in North America, and an awesome spectacle.

When winter rains give way to sunshine, and locals realize that snow is often rain's gift to the mountains in higher climes, skiers and snowboarders take to the slopes. No matter which ski hill is chosen, there are moods to be experienced, happy memories to be captured, and lots of fresh powder to be carved.

A flawless blend of strikingly beautiful young women, gorgeous costumes, and magnificent dancing, the UBC Girlz Bhangra Team sets the bar sky high at the VIBC Festival dance competition. The festival features many folk, Punjabi and fusion dance forms, and exists as a celebration of Bhangra dance, music, and culture.

Living Colour

GLORIA MACARENKO

A Vancouver winter palette is predominantly shades of grey. But, for good reason. Mother Nature provides the perfect minimalist canvas to highlight the colour and energy that define us. Against a sometimes-dreary backdrop: the city explodes in neon along the Granville strip; jewel-toned saris burst impossible hues in the Punjabi market; scarlet lanterns illuminate Chinatown while sparkling gold dragons snake through its streets on lunar New Year; rainbow banners proudly line the streets of the West End; and, brilliantly painted buildings pose for pictures on Granville Island. These are the physical accents of a region rich in vivacity.

Still, even with all these tangible treasures, the true wealth of this city is its people. I have been fortunate enough through my work to come into contact with the incredibly diverse array of individuals who contribute to Vancouver's unique texture. I prepared a special series for the CBC called *Living Colour*, which highlighted the fact that Metro Vancouver has more cross-cultural couples than anywhere else in the country. It is here that east-meets-west and north-meets-south, and there is no question that the children produced from this multicultural gene pool are among the most beautiful in the world. The splendor of the cultural mosaic is no more clearly seen anywhere.

This multifarious mixture of ethnicities also has a palatable plus side, reflected in our food. I love the fact that you can literally eat your way around the world, without ever leaving the city. We are an adventurous lot when it comes to trying new flavours, and Vancouver chefs are constantly challenging our taste buds with innovative combinations of familiar and exotic ingredients. Classic French meets nouveau Japanese, and Latin flavours mingle effortlessly with Mid-Eastern offerings. Fusion seems so common a word that we scarcely stop to wonder what cuisine exactly is being fused. Every menu you come across has a dash of this, a pinch of that, and a sprig of everything else. No matter what your taste, there's plenty of colour to spice up our lives, in the middle of a grey West Coast winter.

No matter what the weather, the lure of Nature at our doorstep is also impossible to resist. Just steps from the city, you can lose yourself in the labyrinth of trails on the University Endowment Lands, and a walk in the rain along the Seawall is always perfect for clearing your mind.

Of course, I live for those moments when the clouds do clear, revealing brilliant blue skies, and fresh snow sparkling on the North Shore Mountains. I bundle up, cradle my cappuccino and stroll blissfully to work across the Burrard Street Bridge, feeling fortunate that this is home.

Gloria Macarenko

Gloria Macarenko

Gloria Macarenko has anchored the news at the Canadian Broadcasting Corporation in Vancouver for more than 20 years. She has received numerous awards for her reporting and broadcasting. She lives with her husband and two sons in Kitsilano.

Charity-of-choice: The Dr. Peter AIDS Foundation
www.drpeter.org

Spring

Riot of Blooms

The garden had always been his—ever since they bought their place in Richmond over thirty years earlier and she had begun chasing him outside to have his smoke. It was him who dragged her to the plant sales and for the spontaneous drives to witness the riot of blooms all over the Lower Mainland. That's what they used to call it then: the Lower Mainland, or Greater Vancouver. Now it's Metro Vancouver.

It was him that had the great love affair with the soil and all things that grew from it. It was him that spent hours and hours, mostly on weekends when he wasn't at work, from early sunrise to the last hint of light, in the garden—planting, weeding, hoeing, and watering, watering, watering. It was always a comfort, though, to have him so close.

He was the one who planned their annual trek to Garibaldi Park, too, a holiday they had enjoyed for over a quarter of a century. They would hike in—him puffing and wheezing—and then camp out by the clear, seemingly bottomless mountain lake. They would meander like kids in a fantasy playground through endless mountain meadows to marvel at the incredible display of alpine flowers, their plant books always at the ready in case they came across a species they didn't recognize. The timing of the summer adventure had to coincide with the bloom of wildflowers that spread their colour over the mountainsides, like a rainbow fire undulating in an alpine breeze.

But now he was gone, and it was up to her to maintain the garden, his garden. He would be both appreciative and astonished at how much of a busy garden bee she had become. The transition from having to, to wanting to, to needing to, had happened easily, within the first weeks of that first spring without him. The experience of labouring in the yard wonderfully filled the void of loneliness. Their only son was back East, raising his family and liking his work. A once or twice a year visit was all there was time for, so the garden had become her *raison d'être*.

Now it was spring, and time to let the plants know that she cherished them. It was also the season of the most work. But that was fine by her, now that she was retired. The work would occupy her time, and steer her mind from any negative thoughts. It would also strengthen her—in body, mind and spirit.

She would have to get in some good soil. That was her starting point. The beds needed to be turned and replenished. She would also add some manure, as she always did, perhaps trying mushroom manure this year. Where did she see that ad? Was it the Boy Scouts who were selling it?

What other ingredients did she need? A list was required, because the rhodies wouldn't care for a dusting of lime. The same with the azaleas and the heathers. They'd be happier with some good old 6-8-6. Oh, so much to do, so much… But she had grown to love it.

Maybe she would start with the VanDusen Plant Sale, where she could get some ideas for new displays in her flowerbeds. The VanDusen Botanical Garden had become a sanctuary throughout her summer garden wanderings. While in the neighbourhood, she could meander around The Quarry at Queen Elizabeth Park. The show the bulbs put on was usually spectacular. Maybe she'd get the nerve to try some Tai Chi behind the Bloedel Conservatory. That is, if there weren't too many tourists looking on. Then there was the UBC Friends of the Garden Plant Sale, along with a tour of Nitobe Memorial Garden to float through the cherry blossoms. Finally, of course, there was always her mid-summer trip out to Chilliwack to see what was new at Minter Country Gardens, perhaps stopping along the way at Century Garden by Deer Lake in Burnaby. And these were just the expeditions she took on her own. Her membership in the Richmond Garden Club gave her a myriad of opportunities to supplement personal outings with visits to astounding exhibitions of plant life in the yards of individual citizens. How they managed to create such incredible beauty was beyond her.

Maybe she would start her list after a cup of Earl Grey and a biscuit just now. Then she could warm up to the spring season with some light pruning and a bit of scratching in the beds. She wondered if the time would ever come when chickens once again ranged freely in people's backyards.

Creating beauty in a personal outdoor space by nurturing and tending a garden is a passion first, and hard work after that. It is a lifestyle shared by all age groups: a senior whose garden near Deep Cove has matured; or a younger dad, who not only wants to spruce up the new homestead by buying a "rhody" at the VanDusen Garden Plant Sale, but who would also love to encourage the beautiful baby he desperately loves to follow his example.

A rampant display of lupin along Richmond's Garry Point causes everyone that uses the area recreationally to pause and be pleasured by the sight.

Tulips are one of those wonderful harbingers of spring, popping up in resident gardens, adorning a vase in the home, or used as a gorgeous prop in a backyard setting.

Unsettling as it may be, fields of tulips in the Fraser Valley are grown for the sole purpose of providing bulbs for the marketplace. The bloom is not sold, instead denied its moment of beauty in the public eye in favour of delighting admirers at a later time, in another place.

From Vancouver's Southlands, near the metropolitan center, to Hope and throughout the Fraser Valley, all things horsy thrive. Riding stables, barns, and paddocks fill out acreages, so that these large hooved mammals are well looked after.

Equestrian excellence is displayed in competitions held at Thunderbird Show Park, while contests of a different kind thrill thousands of rodeo fans. Bulls and broncs buck, and rodeo clowns blend humour with caution at the annual Cloverdale Rodeo.

Save the World

For parents and their children, a casual walk through even a small local park can instigate thought and discussion about a more sustainable environment. For a girl in a more immense greenspace, like Stanley Park, there are infinite questions as the little one surely wonders why those trees are so tall, what they eat, and how they stay so green.

Earth Day in Metro Vancouver is a time for everyone to not only celebrate the natural wonder and beauty of our communities, but to also take stock of what will keep them safe for future generations. For some this can mean taking part in organised cleanups, like a sweep of local sidewalks for trash, or something more personal and subtle, like simply setting aside a special compost bin for the household. In Surrey, it means communing with "Spring", taking away a free sapling to plant at home, and releasing chum salmon into Bear Creek, all in an attempt to encourage our children to think GREEN!

Over the centuries, in countries throughout the world, different cultures have devised different modes of water transportation. In China, the dragon boat originated over two thousand years ago, and races have taken place since that time, with modern dragon boat racing gaining prominence in Hong Kong in 1976. It was also a demonstration sport during Expo '86, and the Rio Tinto Alcan Dragon Boat Festival in Vancouver is now over twenty years young.

The canoes used in British Columbia War Canoe Races today are hybrids of crafts used by various Nations from all along the West Coast. These canoes, like the Chinese boats, were used and raced for centuries.

The tradition is still alive and thriving. Each year at Cultus Lake, thousands of men, women, and children spend the weekend reliving the racing ways of their ancestors, in canoes now specifically designed for the sport.

The power of the symbolism within the images is obvious. An ancient totem, an interior house post from a village of an ancestor figure near Quatsino Sound, and on display in the Museum of Anthropology at UBC, represents legends of another time.

A living totem, dressed in the garb of his Nisga'a forefathers, strides confidently towards the performing of his cultural dances. The pensive looks on the faces of the youth could belie concern or simply share emotion.

Can a child enjoy any purer existence than flying a kite through cherry blossoms with a powder blue sky as a backdrop?

The Dr. Sun Yat-Sen Classical Chinese Garden is a scholar's garden and an authentic representation of a traditional Ming Dynasty creation. Its focus is to emulate the rhythms of Nature, and for anyone who has taken the time to visit, its enchanting spaces do not disappoint.

Berry Beautiful

With the populace understanding that foodstuffs grown close to home are best for everyone and everything, more and more produce is as close as an afternoon drive, depending on what is sought after. By the time fuchsia are prominent in ever-popular plant nurseries, and hydrangea are about to offer their best blush, families can share a bonding experience by picking sun-hot raspberries at a U-Pick farm in Langley. Farm-fresh strawberries, gooseberries, and red and black currants are also on offer. There is no such thing as slim pickings.

For more serious and adventurous foragers, dozens of special spots around Metro Vancouver still boast abundant supplies of wild berries. Patches of blueberries soak up the sun along the banks of the Fraser River and Burrard Inlet, and hikers on Mount Seymour can share thickets of huckleberries with sweet-toothed resident black bears. Meanwhile, Fraser Valley vintners are cashing in on the wealth of berries, as fruit wines of every variety have become de rigueur for newly established farm-wineries.

Spring gardens in Metro Vancouver are sights to behold, presenting themselves as architecturally designed masterpieces, like Century Garden at Deer Lake in Burnaby, whose beauty is undeniable.

For those whose sight has been denied, on the last Friday of every May, approximately a thousand supporters join in the Run for Light to foster awareness and raise funds for programs assisting blind athletes.

Children are introduced to a gamut of bizarre experiences and freakish creatures at the Vancouver International Children's Festival. "The Big Nazo" are just some of these outlandish characters. These oddities are not to be confused with the idiosyncratic nature of some residents, be they a "legion of hard-bitten souls" or not.

A Legion of Hard-Bitten Souls

DAVE GERRY

The first time I laid eyes on Vancouver I was as gobsmacked as the next fellow. The sheer scale of the mountains and the ocean and the trees left me more than a little slack-jawed. I felt absolutely dwarfed by the place, like I'd stepped inside one of those massively brooding Emily Carr paintings.

Once I moved here with my family it took some time for that "supernatural" bloom to come off the rose. Years went by before I was truly comfortable and had a sense of what Vancouver was really all about. It was, and continues to be, so much more than the sum of its topography and vegetation. The people are what makes the place hum.

I was fortunate to have a job that brought me into contact with all types of people from nearly every walk of life. I got to explore their passions by discovering exactly what connected them to Vancouver, and, almost through osmosis, I too felt more connected. I talked with hundreds of artists and craftsmen who expressed themselves through the most natural of materials at hand. These were people who made baskets out of kelp and furniture out of twisted wildwood, and folks who had decided they'd be much happier living on a boat, in a tree house, or even in a cave.

There seemed to be a palpable pioneer spirit just beyond the city's borders, as if great pockets of the population had somehow gotten lost in time. So, I met the gold panners and the bison farmers and the collectors of everything from cast iron frying pans to fire trucks. It seemed to me that many of the so-called eccentrics were having an awfully good time, a much better time than some of their big city brethren.

British Columbia was busy billing itself as "the best place on Earth," but its biggest city seemed to be in a perpetual state of reconstruction. It was noisy and dusty and vehicularly hostile—unless you were at the wheel of a dump truck.

And it was expensive. People were lining up all night to slap down money on a condominium based on a Popsicle stick model—before a single shovel had broken ground. Saner heads and a dampened economy would soon prevail.

Eventually I had to admit that this place was getting under my skin and I began to embrace its singular quirks. I like the fact that people will sit outside at a sidewalk café and sip coffee in a gale. I smile when it snows, because I know there is a legion of hard-bitten souls who will refuse to stop wearing shorts. I think it's admirable, however impractical, that Vancouverites will go to the wall for a tree, that they will drive around trunks in the street (East 12th Avenue), rather than clear-cut a boulevard.

I embrace this city more for its distinctive foibles than its spectacular framework. Sometimes it can be a pretty soggy spot. Far be it for me to rain on the parade.

Dave Gerry

For more than 30 years Dave Gerry has humorously chronicled the contradictions of the human condition in a long list of award winning television feature stories, documentaries and specials.

Charity-of-choice: BC Cancer Foundation
www.bccancerfoundation.com

As it has been for endless summers, children get caught up in fun at the beach, where a waiting raft beckons and entices them to enjoy hours of reckless abandon.

I Began Here and I Will End Here

VICKI GABEREAU

My children are fifth generation Vancouverites. My great-grandmother was born in New Westminster, so I hope that counts. By any measure that isn't such a long time, and we know there have been many before us who walked this land, appreciating and admiring it. Although my family came to British Columbia as foreigners, they soon felt as attached as the original peoples. This province and its largest urban centre are in my blood. Whenever separated by distance, I long for this place—my land and seascape.

I have known almost every square meter of this city. It attracts the very finest of artists, intellectuals and craftsmen. Like all port cities, however, it has an underbelly of restlessness and danger, and is a lure for the desperate and weary. The port of last resort, you could say.

Nevertheless, it charms me that it is possible to find areas where nothing much has changed since the 1950s. Not just the houses that still stand, but the brush and long grass and old train tracks and the river. I am nine again. At that age I roamed my neighbourhood, gone for hours at a time, and without anyone seeming to fret, least of all me. I rode my red bike from Kerrisdale to Southlands two or three times a week, out to UBC for a look around and then down to Spanish Banks or Kitsilano for a tour of the beaches. At least once a week, I would take a bus downtown to a movie with my buddy, Valerie, and then go to the Honey Dew Restaurant for a fuzzy orange drink. In the summer months my grandmother and I would head off to Stanley Park with picnics she had packed, always the same, two pieces of fried chicken, potato salad and a raisin cookie for each of us. My father and mother had a photography business so I remember us, a merry trio, driving all over the Lower Mainland to get scenic shots. Up the mountain, down the other side, up the river and down.

A lot of my childhood was spent at Hastings Park Race Track, where my dad also worked. During the racing season he would get up at 5:00 a.m. and head out to watch the horses at their morning workout. He didn't have to do it, but when I say that he *had* to, I know you'll understand. Sometimes I got to go and hang around with him there. In the dawn light of spring, with the horses excited to be running in the cold morning air, and with steam pumping out of their nostrils, it was, to me, the living end. The steady percussion of hooves hitting the track was as comforting as a heartbeat.

Every city has a rhythm and Vancouver's is a vibrant one. The beat of it has coursed through the generations of my family, the city's pulse now indistinguishable from my own. There is no other place I could *be*. Like my predecessors, I began here and I will end here.

Vicki Gabereau

Vicki Gabereau

Vicki Gabereau, the darling of both national CBC Radio and CTV talk shows with her own programs for decades, has been inducted into the Canadian Broadcast Hall of Fame.

Charity of Choice: Face The World Foundation
www. www.facetheworldfoundation.com

Love your moment

We Sincerely Thank You

It would be arrogant and egotistical for us to think that just the two of us created the vision that appears within the covers of this book. Whether they are those individuals or organizations listed in the credits on the last page, or those noted below, a cast of almost thousands has generously given to us to make this publication possible. If we have erroneously not acknowledged you, our sincerest apologies, but all of you—named or otherwise—know how you helped us. And for those of you who worked with us to capture an image, only to have your shot not make the cut, we are grateful for that investment of time and energy and deeply sorry that space or creativity dictated your photograph's demise. With many a *Thank you*, hugs and kisses, and *We love you*, know that we dearly recognize your contributions.

Our heartfelt appreciation is extended to: our Contributing Writers: Vicki Gabereau, Rick Hansen, Jack Hodgins, Bill Good, Gloria Macarenko, Dave Gerry, and Squire Barnes; our story talent, Darren & Kelly Bromley; our design consultant, Jakub Kania of Jakub Kania Designs; our editor, Robert Marthaller; our website consultant, Eric Welscher-Bilodeau; Bob's family: Megan Herger, Madeline, Carolyn & Michael Fernie, Nyla, Natalie & Paul Crang, and Stephanie Herger—and the whole Fernie, Crang and Herger clans; Ken's mom and sister: Bernice Young & Bonnie Hart; Dave & Dessa Bromley; Angie Chan; The Badgley Clan; Rick Antonson & Tourism Vancouver; Alan McDougall & Raincoast Books and Howard White & Harbour Publishing; David Friesen, Paul Gagné, Jorge Rocha & the Friesen Corporation; Darcy Mainwaring and all the great staff at Xypex Chemical Corporation; and, Mark Oun & Warren Liou for friendship and all things digital.

We would also like to thank: Erin MacMillan & The Rick Hansen Foundation; Dave Reynolds & Chapters; Shari Nitti & News Group; Mark McCurdy, Bob Hoy, Brian Stapleton & MarketPlace IGA; Zac Bailey and Brendan Guy; Robin Braun, Stephanie Fung, Alan Gove & The Vancouver Symphony Orchestra; Brian Paterson & Ballet BC; Tiger Kirkland; Lia Zia, Elenna "Spring" Hope, Angela "The Ta-Daa Lady" Brown, Humna Ahmad, Jasmin Khattar, Sabrine Yoo, Dean Dong, Alexander & Ian Hatch, Stella Meng and Michelle Dow; Jodi Simkin, Hinda Gaate & UBC's Nitobe Garden; Ken Armich; Shara & Aliye Sasmaz; Muriel Clayton and Penny & George Pedersen; Jennifer Hill & Domaine de Chaberton Estate Winery; Keane & Randy Taits and Git–Ts'amiks Nisga'a Dancers; Mark Bernado

& Mount Seymour Resort; Chris Dagenais and William Mbaho & Grouse Mountain Resort; Gord Bell & Gleneagles Golf Course; and, Dean Larsen, Jonathan Davis, Adam Fine, Corey Margolis & Furry Creek Golf & Country Club.

The time invested and assistance given by the following must be acknowledged: Dan Klein, Martin Armitage & David Collings; Laura Ballance, Curve Communications & Cloverdale Rodeo; Melissa Banovich & Fort Langley Historic Site; Chris Pack, Pam Saunders & Thunderbird Show Park; Chaz Romalis, Steve Smith, Drew Mitchell & Cove Bikes; Audry Lochrie & Talking Totem Tours and Mark Point & The Cultus Lake War Canoe Races; BIG NAZO, Ellie O'Day & Vancouver Children's Festival; Hyack Anvil Battery; Anita Webster & The Dragon Boat Festival; Alex Downey & Queen Elizabeth Park staff; Corey Christofferson; Bill McNulty & the BC High School Track & Field Championships volunteers; Jennifer Webb, Bill McLennan & The Museum of Anthropology at UBC; Sandy & Alf Krause & Krause Berry Farms; Peter & Yolande Lissett (and Chlöe), onboard Faem, and Rahilla Khan & West Van Yacht Club; Iain & Susanne Morris, Allison Ford, Laura Fielding Vandergaag and Jason Vandergaag, Dave Jepson, Jamie Horner, Ben Mumford, and Ross Hunter, onboard Mischief; Beth Henschel, Nicole Gibbons, and Laurie Edward; Amanda Wing, Bob Hillman & Vespa Vancouver; Gary Taylor & Metro Vancouver Cricket League; Nathan Van Stone & Vancouver Whitecaps FC; Jacqueline Blackwell & BC Lions; Graham Wall & Vancouver Canadians Baseball; Chelsey Perrella & Vancouver Canucks; Benson Chen, Jason Chan, and Drew Snider & TransLink; Jenn Graham and Lea Carpenter & Easter Seals Wave Regatta; and, Lindsay Chen and Jenny Hubbard & The Drop Zone.

Not to be forgotten are: James Pollard & Theatre Under the Stars; Diane Heal & The Centre for the Performing Arts; Chris O'Grady, Robyn Forrest and Kurt Turchan & *trailpeak*; Paul Carus & Whistler Hydro Broncs; Sonia Andersen & Whistler Pinnacle Hotel; Colin Watt, Dave Garner and Martin Enright; Janka Corewyn, Kits Pool Staff & Vancouver Park Board; Gabe Somjen; Kevin Plastow and Ron Price & The Abbotsford Air Show; Dave Hocking & Vancouver Soaring Association; Greg Kocher & The Diving Locker; Jessica Ruskin and Ewan Anderson; Darcy Campbell & Back In The Saddle Again Riding Club; Don Arnold; Dave Dungey, Brad Fanos, Noah Fanos, Rob Schneeweiss, and

Amber MacDonald, Ashley MacDonald, Amy Townsend, Darren Watts, and Jeff Heatley; Ken Law & MediChair of Sechelt; Sylvia Rayer and Roger Dahlquist; Jean Gelwicks and Peter Lamb; Curtis Hodgson & Byrne Creek Secondary School's Bulldogs Basketball team; Sean Diggins and Caley Vanular; Sukhi Ghuman, Mo Dhaliwal, Vineeta Minhas & UBC Girlz Bhangra Dancers of the Vancouver International Bhangra Celebration Festival; Hana Mehdic, Ivan Lo, Rian Etmanskie, Kalena Conners, Meetra Balooch, Brianna Ko, Bianca Rizzo, Shazya Suleman, Sherry Lin, Katherine Cosco, and Movica Hardjowasito; and, Rebecca Lam and Josh Carpenter.

The perfect finish to any day in any season. While their bovine companion obliviously enjoys the lush spoils of the Valley, two youngsters end evening chores with a swing against a perfect backdrop of magnificent mountains and the bold blue sky.

Copyright © 2009 by SummerWild Productions

All rights reserved. No part of this publication my be reproduced, stored in a retrieval system, or transmitted in any form or by any means, electronic, mechanical, photocopying, recording, or otherwise, without prior written permission from the publisher, or in the case of photocopying or other reprographic copying, through access via a license from a licensing body, such as the Canadian Copyright Licensing Agency—except by a reviewer, who may quote brief passages and use no more than two images in a review.

Library and Archives Canada Cataloguing in Publication

Herger, Bob
Vancouver, living the moment: a photographic essay of Metro Vancouver /
Bob Herger, photographer; Ken Budd, text

ISBN 978-0-9811933-0-4

1. Vancouver (B.C.)—Pictorial works. 2. Vancouver (B.C.).
I. Budd, Ken, 1942- II. Title.

FC3847.37.H46 2009   971.1'33050222   C2009-900751-7

Production Credits

Executive Producer: Ken Budd
Photographer: Bob Herger

Writers: Ken Budd, Jack Hodgson, Rick Hansen, Bill Good, Squire Barnes,
    Gloria Macarenko, Dave Gerry and Vicki Gabereau

Editor: Robert Marthaller

Designers: Ken Budd, Bob Herger and Jakub Kania of Jakub Kania Designs

Printed in Canada by Friesens Corporation in Altona, Manitoba
Print Consultant: Jorge Rocha

The Garda Silk paper used in this publication is old-growth-free, chlorine-free, and has been harvested utilizing sustainable forestry practices.

Publisher:

SummerWild Productions
340 Rayfield Road, Gibsons, B.C. V0N 1V5

Photo Credits

Kevin Plastow and The Abbotsford International Air Show (Page #51, smallest image)
Bob Frid & Vancouver Whitecaps FC (Page #33, smallest image)
Courtesy of TransLink (Page #73, smallest image)
Bob Frid & The BC Lions (Page #81, both images)
Jeff Vinnick & The Vancouver Canucks (Page #102, both images)
Darren Stone & The Victoria Times Colonist for Jack Hodgins' liner notes photo
Mark Oun for Bob Herger's photo on the dust jacket

Vendor & Distributor Enquiries and Volume Discount Information

Contact the publisher through the following website address if you wish to carry *Living the Moment* in your store, to distribute it to outlets that you have contracts with, or should you wish to use the book as a corporate gift for preferred clients, or to give to your clan!

www.summerwild.ca